All Roads Lead to Peace

Juwon Ogungbe

Afrocentric Creatives

Copyright © 2024 Juwon Ogungbe

All rights reserved

This book is sold subject to the condition that it shall not, by way of trade or otherwise be lent, resold, hired out or otherwise circulated without the publisher's prior consent in any form of binding or cover other than that in which it is published and without a similar condition including this condition being imposed on the subsequent purchaser.

Cover design - Marva Jackson Lord (Griots Arts)

Photo of author - Dennis Low

Contents

Title Page
Copyright
Introduction
Waiting for the guru ... 3
Playfulness and going gaga ... 5
An inner conversation ... 6
Meaning ebbs and flows ... 7
Dining out on an idea ... 9
Presence in passing ... 11
Change and acceptance. ... 12
Too late to recreate. ... 13
Your personal gig ... 14
Who owns the image? ... 15
Sharing World Heritages ... 16
Embracing the shifts ... 17
Access and mind games ... 19
In and out of parallel universes ... 21
Me and we in expression ... 23
Reminders of our roots ... 25
Keen to follow advice. ... 27

Music and the psyche	29
Who is taken in by the show?	31
Feeling safe	33
Reflection and Documentation	35
The Call of the Divine	36
Psychic Phones	37
A winning style	39
Added Cultural Value	41
Proselytising for a style	43
Awakening	45
Swings and roundabouts of creation	46
In with the new	48
Hearing and adhering	50
A job becomes a chore.	52
Tips about those quips	53
Home grown grass.	54
Juwon's Bandcamp page goes live!	55
Angles of a narrative	57
Candlelight	58
I ain't playing	60
Festive Event	62
Time to reflect.	63
The best possible taste	64
Updating customs	66
Choices and impact	68
Being romantic about aesthetics	69
Needs and acceptance	71
Seeking approval.	73

Are minds changing?	75
Rapt attention	76
Favours and the long game	78
Samedi is Saturday	80
Farewell, addiction.	81
What does the image say to you?	83
Reserving the right to morph	84
Authenticity from Africa	86
Discoveries about Destiny	88
Hearing Voices	90
Light and the downside	91
Gliding with Swans	92
Perception and Baggage	93
Experience and Process	95
Ode to an enduring friendship	96
About The Author	99

Introduction

The Lockdown phases during the COVID pandemic gave many people an opportunity to slow down and listen to their inner voices. Several years before 2020, I found myself in a situation where I had to do something similar.

I was working in an American university, living in a secluded cottage and surrounded by thickets of shrubbery. The experience was a far cry from the life I was accustomed to as a Londoner, where I could go out at any time of the day or night.

Shortly before the Lockdown, Marva Lord - a great friend and creative collaborator of mine, drew my attention to a phone app that could be used to make podcasts. I downloaded the app onto my phone, hoping to find a moment to get to grips with how to make it work.

When the Lockdown kicked in, suddenly I had a lot of time on my hands. The phone app was easy to use and in the twinkling of an eye, Multiverse, my podcast series was born. I was already well practised at being alone and sitting still, from my American experience, so I started making short weekly episodes of the show.

I sent out the episodes on my social media profile pages and to my contacts in WhatsApp. The process hasn't involved a lot of back and forth communication between the listeners and me, but there have been times when friends complained that I didn't send them an episode, so I can only assume that some people like to hear from me.

Jack Lookman - an old school mate of mine from King's College Lagos, suggested that the podcast scripts could be turned into a book. His brainwave was a precious gift.

Back in my days of seclusion in the USA, I attended a session with a psychic medium who told me I could write a book. In that conversation, the medium spoke of the potential subject matter for said book and ended the message saying 'All roads lead to peace'.

Now, I have the pleasure of bringing together the essence of the medium's message and Jack Lookman's gift.

This book features some of the earliest podcast scripts, all together in one volume. The podcasts have provided spaces for me to shed light on nooks and crannies in my psychological hinterland. I hope that readers will be inspired by the range of themes and topics covered in this book to feel free to allow themselves to roam and explore beyond the confines of what anyone else might expect of them, especially based on their cultural backgrounds.

In a stream of consciousness/freewheeling manner, this book aims to give readers a glimpse into my idea of what a free spirit can be or do.

Hoping to give you reading pleasure, I urge you to reflect on possibilities for yourself. My wish is for you and me to find peace of mind in our ongoing journeys.

Juwon Ogungbe

November 2024

All Roads Lead to Peace
Juwon Ogungbe

Waiting for the guru

"Why did you choose to be seen out and about with someone who cannot see?" I was once asked. "Because he's a friend of mine and I like to help him by taking him out on an exeat day from school" was my reply.

"Don't you know there are lots of people like that begging on the streets?" My inquisitor fumed.

"Yes, I know" was my response.

"So, you chose to do what you felt within?"

This was the cue for the koboko to be unleashed. A koboko is a whip made from cow hide.

Someone was going to get whipped, yet another time.

When is it right to follow your instincts? And when is it wrong?

In a rehearsal room, a group of theatre makers discussed the pro and cons of diversity and equal opportunities.

One participant mentioned the fact that people of some ethnic heritages are often overlooked in public debates about the issues, while others are regularly featured in media reports.

Another group member asked the complainant to give examples of moments when folks of her heritage had drawn mass attention to the injustices they frequently face.

She said in response that people of her background were not often encouraged to express disagreement with any instructions or orders imposed by authority figures, or the status quo.

"How do you expect anyone to know how you're feeling, if you don't say anything?" She was asked.

She didn't answer because she needed time to reflect.

What do we do to each other in the name of 'home training'?

Playfulness and going gaga

"There's a method to his madness."

How often have you heard this remark?

Legendary figures make reputations that generate money for others, based on presenting questionable mental health as something glamorous, or spectacular.

I had an encounter once with someone who fits this description. At a well-attended public event, he wore a Nigerian agbada, which looked fine, but he chose to accessorise it with a toy crown.

From a conversation I had with a friend, I learnt that this same legendary figure once gate crashed an office business meeting, went right up to the host, unpeeled a banana, stuffed it in the host's mouth and then left the room, without uttering a word.

The legend obviously had some talent, but there was something amiss about the way that people put up with his antics.

He was a survivor. Not everyone in such a predicament manages to prevail for so long.

Tales abound of people losing their lives, possibly because others choose to regard their ill health as entertainment of the car crash variety.

With the world having emerged from a reflective phase, does this offer food for thought?

An inner conversation

Someone sent me a striking video clip on WhatsApp. Interestingly, it was initially posted by someone who lives in Nigeria. I've mentioned this fact because the video was shot somewhere in the UK.

In a corner shop, customers queued up to pay for goods they wanted to buy.

One of them was a casually dressed man who was recognised by the shopkeeper when he arrived at the counter.

The two of them exchanged pleasantries and after a short while, it became clear that the casually dressed man was actually very famous. One could describe him as infamous in some quarters.

This man is not renowned for sensitivity in dealing with people of colour, yet he seemed perfectly comfortable in this corner shop which was full of them.

After finishing the transaction, he posed for selfies with men and women of a particular ethnic minority heritage, before getting on his bike and cycling away.

Is it possible that he likes the company of people of some races, but not of other ones? If so, is there a clear way of describing the mindset that chooses to exclude folks of one or two races from participating in making choices that affect us all?

Meaning ebbs and flows

When I use the expression "neither fish nor fowl". I'm usually thinking about someone or something difficult to quantify.
The term comes to mind when I think about heritages as well.

There are many of us who live in British cities within cultures and traditions that could be described as hybrids. This is because we have created our own values, beliefs and social codes that are not the same as those of the majority ethnic communities.

Someone I know very well was bullied a lot as a young man, for not thinking or communicating like a typically patriarchal Yoruba man, even though he grew up in North London.

We all look for solutions when we're confronted with problems. This guy decided to opt for fitting in with the marginalised Yoruba subculture in London.

It was interesting to observe the process he went through, trying to learn as many Yoruba proverbs as possible to use in conversations, since this mode of communication is regarded as wise.

Obviously, we never fully become anyone that wasn't already part of who we are, so he speaks with a curious turn of phrase that enables him to feel safe in the circles he moves in.

Maybe a time will come when his brand of London Yoruba paternalism will be the standard way to function. But there again, someone else might come up with something that suits everyone better.

Isn't it much easier to simply be who we really are?

Dining out on an idea

Several years ago, I was involved in a tour with a group that performed my music in venues all over England.

The group and the tour came into being because of an agreement between a promoter and me. I took charge of the music, (naturally, since over 90% of the repertoire was created by me), but the promoter had some creative input, especially regarding selecting some of the performers in the ensemble.

There was one group member who had long conversations with me during our coach journeys on the tour. We spoke a lot about the central idea of the music we were performing.

In the arrangements I created for the group, individual performers were given space to bring something extra from their cultural backgrounds. It was agreed that the idea worked well.

At the end of the tour, I left the UK for a long while to work in the USA. In the time I was away, some of the performers decided they were going to opt out of doing any more performances with the ensemble, even though we were gradually building up audience support.

When I returned to London, I got in touch with everyone in the group. The person who had the long conversations with me during the tour would not answer any phone calls and wouldn't respond to any messages.

Not too long after that, it became clear that this person wanted to run with the essence of the ideas that we discussed, to use in a different setting. A few insiders noticed this clear sequence of events.

Nobody owns anyone else. People who are good at generating interesting ideas usually come up with other ones. Those who feed off creative people like parasites can have their moments in the sun, but after a while, they still need to come up with new ideas.

Presence in passing

In the heritage of my forebears, there is a tradition of giving the spirits of ancestors a chance to contribute to our continuous assessment of values. The ancestral spirits get their moment during the Egungun Masquerade festivals that happen in Yoruba communities every year.

For those who don't know what this looks like, there is lots of footage on YouTube and on similar platforms.

When the Masquerades do their rounds, we don't get to think much about who those ancestors were as individuals. They take on new identities when they appear.

A person who has recently passed away is usually vivid as his or herself in most of our memories, however.

He or she might have been notable for having skills, talents or character traits. The person might have lived through an era that many remember with fondness. Maybe he or she might have been an active participant in uplifting our spirits.

How many of us can sustain that sort of contribution from early adulthood through into old age? This is not an easy question to answer.

Maybe we can only make magic for limited lengths of time.

Change and acceptance.

The body knows when the game is up. At least my body does. It always tells me when I've come to the end of a phase or cycle. It's usually time to cultivate new habits.

Sometimes it's hard to give things up. I go through a period of numbness, followed by mourning for the loss of the ritual. Is it because I think of fading youthfulness? Who knows?

Further down the line, I look back and wonder why I kept on repeating the same patterns of behaviour for so long.

At one point I was away from home for a long period of time. I got to meet several new acquaintances where I went, but I was isolated most evenings. When I returned to my home, I started forming new habits. People commented often on how much I had changed.

I don't weigh the pros and cons of change. It is bound to happen.

Someone once gave me the impression that he felt I changed things too often. We all know what makes us feel fulfilled. Some of us need life to be dynamic and flowing, even if it means we don't fit into the standard idea of being successful.

The present moment offers everyone a chance to reflect about the sort of changes we would like to see happening.

As the song says, "everything must change; nothing remains the same".

Too late to recreate.

What does an "easing up" of the lock down entail? Can we simply go back to doing things the way they were done before?

The changes we're going through are like nothing I've seen in a lifetime. We all need to learn new ways of functioning and relating to each other.

I've been told that my mindset on this situation is too bleak. There seems to be a fear that many of us will come a cropper because of the changes.

Is it possible that some of us are holding on too tightly to the old ways? What would happen if we invested more energy in thinking of new ways to carry on with our lives?

I sense that we have closed a chapter. It's time to turn a new page.

There are no guarantees or certainties, but we can do better if we face the reality of what is happening.

Perhaps there will be a time when we'll look back at the way things were, then at this transitional period and we might wonder if we made the best use of the time.

Your personal gig

Aesop was a great storyteller. There has been some speculation that his name was derived from Ethiope, as in Ethiopian. Who knows if Aesop was of African heritage? One of his most memorable fables is *The Town Mouse and the Country Mouse.* I'm going to assume that most readers know the story. I find it useful in relation to some myths that are peddled about musicians of African heritage who live in Europe.

There was a time when all the World Music followers believed that Paris was the hub for African derived music. We were led to believe that there was something magical about the city and the music making going on there.

Someone I know who was involved in selling this notion once told me a story about the first time he visited the city of lights. He was rudely awakened by what he saw.

At the airport, he saw Africans being led away somewhere in chains. They were probably illegal immigrants, but the image was somehow at odds with the tales that were told so often.

The grass might appear to be greener elsewhere, but everything begins from within.

Who owns the image?

A successful record producer told a story of the inspiration behind one of his hit records.

Apparently, the artist showed him a photo of someone renowned for his style and flair – a great influencer. He said he wanted the record to sound like the look of the photo. The rest is history.

I thought of images that could inspire me in a similar way. One photo came to mind, of a famous African sportsman who collaborated with a Parisian fashion house.

The photo was beautifully evocative. I don't even need to see it again to remember what I liked.

Because of this, I went to the sportsman's Instagram page, to see if there were more photos to inspire me. He has a fine page, with lots of nice photos, but nothing that reminded me of the first one I saw.

It made me wonder about what people see in each other. The stories we tell ourselves are most important for us, but they don't always have much to do with anyone else's reality.

Sharing World Heritages

In my days as an emerging artist, older Black musicians I met often complained about being shafted one way or another in the record business.

From many reports, they went into partnerships and collaborations with White musicians of their age group and would share ideas in jam sessions and other musical explorations.

At some point in most of the stories, the White musicians would attract support from influential figures in the business and many of the Black musicians would be dropped as the act moved on to the next level of market value.

Black musicians of my age group have probably had different experiences. Maybe we weren't as trusting as the guys who came before us. Perhaps we learnt more Intellectual Property Law on the way.

We encountered other barriers, however. How come there wasn't a top league Black led group in the Black Rock era of the 1990s, for example?

Those of us who stayed the course came to realise that we could do anything we wanted if we were willing to pay the price for not toeing the line.

A lot of people are speaking up about race-based obstruction now.

Embracing the shifts

Starting from Monday, the 15th of June 2020, it will be compulsory to wear face covering on public transport in England.

This is one regulation that I find difficult to comply with, but I will do so if I use the trains or buses.

Quite a few people I know have been resistant to other changes brought about by the Covid-19 disruption. Some have not ventured into using video conferencing tools, for example.

I performed an online song recital last weekend. The event was successful, and I enjoyed the process. After the concert, I heard from some associates who wanted to know it went. I asked why they didn't tune in.

One person said, 'I could see your ugly mug, but I couldn't hear anything'.

'Did you switch on your audio?' I asked.

I didn't get a coherent response to this question. So, I probed further.

'Haven't you been in a Zoom meeting? Where have you been all this time?'

The answer I got was 'I'm self-employed; why would I be in a Zoom meeting?'

The conversation was becoming odd, so I said 'I'm self-employed as well. What has 'being in a Zoom Meeting' got to do with being self-employed?'

As Bob Dylan said – 'The times they are a changing'. Is it really that hard to get with the programme?

Access and mind games

Why do people tell stories, or listen to them? I think it's because we use narratives as guides, maps, or points of reference for dealing with life. We want to solve problems, or feel better when we're sad, for example.

It has been stated many times that *Every picture tells a story.* We also hear sounds and associate them with one tale or another.

A friend invited me to a performance he was taking part in. The event was presented in a beautiful modern Church building. The location and setting gave me high hopes for what I was going to hear.

In fact, the acoustics of the space were weird. The pianists played well, but a lot of the sound frequencies were lost in the auditorium. It is possible that the instrument might have sounded better if it had been placed somewhere different in the hall, but no one had bothered to experiment with this option before the audience arrived.

My friend probably thought I was nitpicking when I told him it would have been better for the show to be presented in a hovel with good acoustics.

Those of us who dedicate our lives to telling stories sometimes end up not seeing the wood for the trees. It's as if the reason for all the energy expended is to acquire enhanced status for ourselves. But it's the constant process of telling more stories that really counts for something.

I'm not suggesting that it isn't important to make people aware that the story is available to be read, seen, or heard. It's simply a case of making sure we get our priorities right.

In and out of parallel universes

Time, space, and boundaries take on new dimensions on Social Media platforms. The immediacy of direct messaging or conversations on a thread can create an artificial sense of closeness.

Once when I was touring, I contacted a friend who lives in city outside of London. We agreed to meet up at the event I was involved in presenting.

Face to face in the auditorium, we tried to recall the last time we had seen each other in person. I was amazed when I realised the last time was 24 years before that encounter. Regular social media chats had given me a misleading impression.

I've made many new friends during the lockdown season. When I get a friendship request, I go to the person's profile page to see who she or he is before deciding to accept.

Recently, I've had an odd experience with someone who describes himself as a healer amongst other things. He started a conversation with me and in no time at all, he demanded that I include his phone number on another platform. I don't respond very well to bossy individuals, so I was polite about ignoring his commands.

Due the nature of my work, I am easily reachable by phone, so he managed to find my details. Ever since then he has tried to bully me into talking to him on the phone. I haven't decided to block him yet.

Times are hard for many of us, and we are all thinking of ways and means to survive and thrive. Is this fellow a hypnotist? Even if he is, why does he think he can have his way, communicating with no semblance of charm in his manner?

Me and we in expression

I count myself lucky to have known what it felt like to be 'the only Black person in the village' at an early age, along with knowing the feeling of being surrounded by only people of my race and heritage for miles and miles, also as a childhood experience.

Many of my contemporaries only experienced one of these ways of being, or the other. Those who know both sides of the coin have a sensibility that is not often given much airtime.

In my young adulthood, I encountered many Londoners who happen to share the same skin colour as me, who didn't understand the nuances of living in a truly Black world.

They were frustrated when I didn't agree with them about certain issues pertaining to Black or African Diaspora identity. Was I an Uncle Tom? They would have been happy to label me as such, but I was also familiar with aspects of several African heritages, based on firsthand knowledge. This concept was too complex for them to grasp.

Those were the days when Apartheid was still legal in South Africa. I had interesting experiences with White, Coloured and Black South Africans. Some of them were confused by my sensibility.

I knew enough about Eurocentric attitudes to hold my own, yet I am as dark skinned as they come, knew three of my grandparents well and could easily glide into 'passing' for an African who had never left Africa.

There were some narrow escapes from scrapes that could have been violent, for this reason.

Obviously, the problems were more to do with the emotional baggage carried by my detractors than me, but I was young and callow. I would deal with those situations differently today, knowing what I know.

I wonder if similar layers of cultural misunderstanding still hover around us nowadays.

Reminders of our roots

My homemaking skills are Spartan. Any piece of visual art to be found in my living space was probably a gift. I am not an art collector by any stretch of the imagination, but I enjoy visiting art galleries and I often draw inspiration from the shows I see.

I even composed a song cycle called *After hours in the African Gallery,* which was inspired by objects I saw in The British Museum. One song from that cycle has now morphed into a short piece for violin and piano which is featured in an entry level anthology of pieces by Black composers.

One exhibition that remains vivid in my memory after a couple of decades is the *'Africa: Art of a continent'* show that was presented by the Royal Academy of Arts in London as part of the *Africa'95 Festival.*

The range of works on display was breathtaking. Some parts of the show would have been more suitable for a craft fair, but others, such as the tall wooden statues of warriors that were created for tombs, hushed many viewers into awe and reverence.

A friend of mine was troubled by the show, because his Walkman stopped working, just as he stepped into the front courtyard of the Royal Academy. There was nothing I could say to convince him that the battery power died as a coincidence.

Many folks of African descent associate the images created by African artists of yesteryears with rituals, ceremonies, and the wielding of supernatural powers.

Some art works were probably kept in temples, shrines, mansions, and palaces, but very few folks know much about the thinking behind the creativity.

Is it healthy to regard our cultural inheritance as potentially harmful?

Keen to follow advice.

Only a few years ago, I was invited to work with the chorus of an orchestra from an African country. At that point in time the full ensemble was described in media circles as the only one that featured solely Black musicians. I'm not sure whether this was a fact or not, since there easily could have been such a group in the USA, but this orchestra was certainly unusual. I had a great time working with the orchestra's choir. They had a great sound and were friendly people. To be honest, I thought the singers were the best feature of the ensemble when I heard them in concert.

Fast forwarding only a few years later and now there is a lot more activity coming from people of African descent who sing or play art music. Who would have thought I could have instant messaging conversations with emerging young African classical musicians who are currently grounded due to Covid-19 restrictions and living in remote provincial African towns and cities?

A way of life that once felt like being out on a limb is suddenly becoming the flavour of the moment. Not sticking out like a sore thumb feels odd. It will take some getting used to.

Now, it is fine for this energy to focus primarily on performing the Eurocentric canon. The ethos of playing and singing art music in orchestras, chamber groups and solo performances originated in Europe, without a doubt.

What is going to happen to this new African movement in the long term?

One can only hope that new African derived idioms and genres will emerge. We have our own ways and means of communicating that are not always the same as those of our non-African counterparts.

I'm looking forward to hearing new sounds and approaches. Maybe we'll even entice African audiences into engaging with our music on a grassroots level.

Music and the psyche

Someone I know from my days as a university student happened to be online when I was on Facebook Live recently. He stopped by to listen to what I had to say.

When I finished the vlog presentation, I found that he had left me some comments. He said I had come a long way. This remark got me thinking about my creative journey.

I never found a community of musicians to belong to. I believe this is because I have something to express that is unique and not easy to compartmentalise.

Many years ago, I read an autobiography of someone who made a lot of money out of the record business as a manager. He had a great sense of humour, told a lot of stories that some might regard as salacious about the music business of London in the swinging sixties, and even took a long break, only to return in the 1980s to make even more money.

He claimed that successful recording acts could claim to be quirky, but in the long run they couldn't really be musically original or different. They had to make sounds that somehow fitted in with the trends of a given moment.

When I reflect about the sounds and trends I've heard in my time as an artist, I'm inclined to agree with him. This doesn't mean that there can't be any exceptions to prove the rule, of course.

Some artists are not cut out to be like that. They need to be themselves and they create what Ray Charles described as 'honest music'. I like to think I'm one of those.

On that long journey that my university peer alluded to, I have explored and experimented with a wide variety of sounds, textures, and approaches. Quite a few people I met on the way have dropped out for various reasons, but I'm still around. Doing what I do, being who I am.

Many folks have asked me why I haven't just cashed in my chips and toed the line. I don't think I have it in me to be like that.

I guess a lot depends on one's reasons for being an artist in the first place.

Who is taken in by the show?

Recent debates about the doctors who assembled in Washington DC in front of an official building to make claims about having found a cure to Covid-19 remind me of a childhood experience.

In New Barnet, where I lived at the time, it wasn't very often that a funfair came to town. On a memorable occasion, the local park was taken over by a visiting fair. Naturally, children in the neighbourhood were excited and wanted to see the spectacle.

I spoke to my foster mother about the event, and she gave me half a crown to spend there. I guess half a crown in those days would be about 25p now.

In the park, attention was drummed up for a sight that was presented as the highlight of the fair. It was a chance to see 'The Queen of the Carnival'. How much would it cost to see her? Exactly half a crown.

Taken in by the promises of the fairground barkers, I paid my money to see the Queen of the Carnival. Even as a 7-year-old, I could tell that this was simply a middle-aged woman, dressed up in fancy clothes. Was she a fairy godmother? Would she sing, dance, or perform magic with the wave of a wand? The answer, sadly, was no. She simply stood on a spot, being the Queen of the Carnival. I lost interest in her mystique rather swiftly.

Then I noticed other things I would have preferred to spend my money on, such as candy floss and toffee apples. I went back home to tell my foster mother about the uninteresting Queen of the Carnival and asked if she would give me some money for sweets. She refused, wisely, saying I had half a crown, and it was all I was going to get. I had made my choice. I remember feeling upset about it at the time.

Those doctors who assembled in Washington DC to make videos that were widely circulated around the world should be held to account if their claims turn out to be unreliable.

Feeling safe

It was my first visit to Lagos in 18 years. I had done my research regarding suitable times of the day to arrive at the airport, etc, but in the end I arrived in the evening. My chaperone was in the right place, at the right time, so there were no issues with travelling through the city at night. In my early teenage years, I used to travel on my own from one end of Lagos to another, every day. For those who know Lagos, I would travel from Racecourse, (where I went to school) to Ikeja, so I didn't regard myself as newbie in town.

What I wasn't prepared for, was the extent to which things had changed since I was last there.

We arrived in Obalende, which is quite close to my old school. A room had been booked in a guest house, just for one evening.

It was past midnight, but it felt like no one was going to sleep. Under a bridge that functioned as a bus terminus and a hub for wayfarers, throngs of people were wide awake. Street traders plied their wares. I suddenly felt fearful and unsafe.

I spoke about this feeling with my chaperone later. He had visited the UK on one occasion. He asked me *'How is this different to throngs of people at London Victoria Station?'* I had a clear sense of why it felt different. I said to him:

At Victoria Station, people look like they're on their way to another destination. They could be waiting for trains, but you could tell what they were aiming to do. At Obalende, people were just hanging out, with no clear intentions.

It is possible that my perception was jaundiced or prejudiced about Obalende, under the bridge at midnight, but my premonitions about my visit to Lagos were not unfounded, as I discovered further down the line.

If I have learnt to trust anything in my time, my instincts will always come first. We can wish things were different, but intuition usually points us in the right direction.

Reflection and Documentation

It took me a couple of decades to accept that some folks are best kept as friends, but not as collaborators on work related projects.

Time after time, I would take the initiative and set the ball rolling in a particular direction and then I would be enticed yet again into giving a particular work partnership another roll of the dice.

Now I think I understand the dynamics of compatibility in teamwork.

There was one instance when I found myself caught up in making this same mistake in presenting a show, and some other friends turned up with a highly skilled camera crew and sophisticated equipment to film the event.

We ended up using the occasion as an opportunity to film interviews and solo performances that have stood the test of time. I guess we would have needed to book a location for filming etc if I hadn't accepted the initial offer.

Having said this, I would be foolish to keep on putting myself in compromised positions. *'Countless times bitten; even more times shy'* is now my watchword.

The Call of the Divine

Intuition has a funny way of letting you know when a chapter of life is coming to an end; and another one is about to start. The Covid-19 related lockdown has certainly worked like that in my life. A lot of circumstances were neatly stacked up, to make it easy for me to accept the restrictions of the period.

I was even prepared for the feeling of being isolated. I had a practice run several years ago in the USA.

At that point in time, I stayed alone in a bungalow, surrounded by thickets of shrubbery and trees. Deer, antelopes, and other animals roamed freely in the area. Out on the main road, there were no streetlights or pavements to walk on. Motorists drove at night, not expecting to see any pedestrians. Doing my grocery shopping had to be planned like a military expedition. If I didn't catch the right bus, I would be stranded for up to 90 minutes.

So, the lockdown was like a rerun of a previous series of events for me. It gave me a chance to look within and become productive in ways I hadn't been in a long time.

For someone used to frequent travelling on underground trains, to be in London and not step inside one for over 14 weeks was very interesting. Now that things are supposedly easing up, the idea of getting around in London the way I used to feels almost alien.

But the powers that be are calling for business to return its usual pace. How is that going to happen?

Psychic Phones

It's been a week now since I learnt about the demise of friend of mine. This was someone I knew very well over several decades and there was even a time when we lived in the same house.

In the reports that carried the sad news, it was said that he passed away two years before I found out. For several reasons, this information wasn't disclosed to his friends till now.

Occasionally I attend a Spiritualist Church, where a psychic medium gives a demonstration. I hadn't done this frequently in ages. I might have gone twice in the last couple of years.

Both times, the medium had a message for me. One of them spoke of someone like a family member who mentioned that I was a natty dresser and alluded to how often I would iron my trousers. The message didn't resonate with me at the time because I couldn't think of any family member on the Spirit Plane who would refer to this detail.

Now that I know about this close friend having been on the Spirit Plane since 2018, the message makes more sense. When we stayed together, it was also with a younger sibling of mine. I used to wear specially made African outfits in those days, which attracted a lot of attention. Most of the trousers I wore were baggy, and like those made famous by MC Hammer – a hugely successful pop rap artiste of that era.

Can I remember the rest of the message? Not now. I had no idea that my friend was on the other side.

Sadly, the last time we tried to have a phone conversation, his phone was faulty, and it wasn't possible to make head or tail of what he was saying.

The chronology of these events is a bit too hazy to work out now. My gut tells me however, that it was my friend who was trying to reach me through the medium.

A winning style

Nigerians often refer to the way they bring up their offspring as 'home training'. I can see the link between this turn of phrase and the way Yorubas describe it. I'm not sure about the other indigenous languages and what they would say.

I like to think I was given a good home training by my parents and carers. We were taught to treat adults and elders with respect. This was okay with me, but admiration was something I kept as a personal gift. Only I could decide which adults or elders I regarded as worthy of being admired.

To be very honest, there were very few elders that bowled me over in such a manner, so it was quite special to meet a Nigerian scholar at a symposium in Cambridge who had the 'wow' factor, in my opinion.

When I first saw this man, he delivered a keynote address in a Cambridge University college without any prepared notes. Even though he apologised for winging it, I found his talk to be erudite, urbane, and highly engaging.

He was a natty dresser, friendly and approachable and always seemed to be genuinely interested in what I was up to, after I was introduced to him. At another Symposium in Cambridge, a few years later, he took me out to lunch, and I had a fabulous time, shooting the breeze with a Nigerian man of my parents' generation who was seemingly clued up about cutting edge trends and developments in the arts. Sadly, that was the last time I saw him, and our email conversations were not as warm as it was to deal with him, face to face.

I've just noticed a tweet by one of his offspring, paying tribute to him on his birthday and I want to doff my cap in respect.

Are there others like him out there? I haven't met them.

Added Cultural Value

Several years ago, I was involved in a project put together by an orchestra to highlight the works of composers of African descent. My job was to lead groups of young people in creating group compositions inspired by the works featured in a concert programme that was to be performed in a major concert hall.

Several aspects of the experience were tricky to deal with, but I like to regard myself as a trouper, so I rolled with the punches and did what I had to do.

One of the pieces featured in the programme was a celebrated work by a composer who is perceived as a patriarchal figure amongst African musicians. This piece is especially recognisable because the composer included fragments from a well-known Yoruba folk song in one of its movements.

The project required me to stay in digs, away from home and there were several days of concentrated activity. After doing my work on the first day, I left the venue so the orchestra could rehearse the programme.

I had a chance to socialise with some of the musicians on the morning after the rehearsal. Some of them expressed contentious opinions about the well-known African piece. They were keen to share their views.

As far as they were concerned, the work was not an effective or successful representation of African music. They felt the composer's attempts to use a western orchestral sound world somehow neutered the music's African traits, thereby weakening the symbolic value of the work.

In subsequent years, I have heard performances, participated in concerts, and composed pieces of my own that are likely to be categorised as African art music. In some cases, the pieces were highly effective in making an impact. There were others that suffered from the composers aspiring towards respectability on non-African terms.

There is a growing community of young Africans who are developing skills as orchestral musicians. It makes sense that they should play the standard repertoire as they embark on their artistic journeys, but it seems to me that they need to have a canon of repertoire that they know, understand, and perform better than anyone else.

Who will bring the African composers and instrumentalists together, to sing from the same hymn sheet?

Proselytising for a style

In my mind, career paths cross and uncross in synergy, but I've had to explain my processes to quite a few collaborators who misunderstood my intentions.

Classical singing is one of my favourite pursuits. Like any other activity, if you focus on doing it a lot, it becomes part of your life. Similarly, I love creating music for theatre. When I first started out, my aim was to focus on creating my own music theatre work. As it happened, friends and associates from the world of spoken word theatre asked me to join their teams to work on other shows. I remained on this path for the best part of twenty years.

Meanwhile, my singing teacher attended my music theatre shows and encouraged me to join an opera training programme. Getting used to the process took a while, but eventually it added another string to my bow.

In more recent times, when I created and made demonstration recordings of music for a spoken word theatre production, my collaborators - not understanding the way my mind works, would hear my voice, and assume that I intended to bring classical singing into their productions. In other words, they couldn't separate the songs I composed from the sound of my voice.

Quite often, I would have to explain that the songs would sound different when sung by actors who were not classical singers.

I accept now that I must bring my skills and talents together to create the performing arts genre that makes the most of my experiences. It isn't something that can be described in words. The creative work needs to be done and shared before folks will know what it is.

Is this the birth of a new genre?

Awakening

When I was a child, I heard about a famous politician who was renowned for being hostile to people who had a different skin colour to his. He was partially responsible for inviting people from Britain's colonies to migrate to the heart of the Empire, to help in the nation's efforts to rebuild, after World War 2. Why did he become an advocate for xenophobia further down the line? There might be a historian who has written about this subject with inside knowledge, but most of us don't know the answer to this question.
A couple of decades later, the same politician denied expressing any racist or xenophobic views in public at any point in his career. This stance seemed confusing to folks like me who remembered him from our childhoods.

What I didn't understand was how easy it is for some people to be duplicitous communicators.

In recent times, there have been reports about a controversial public figure forming a new political party to 'reclaim values.'

This new party has sponsors. Presumably we can look forward to a lot of gaslighting in public discourse about diversity and equal opportunities.

The movement's arrowhead will probably deny any intentions to stir up race-based unrest, but the jury is still out in this regard.

Swings and roundabouts of creation

I have a long history of finding myself in situations where people have come together, ostensibly to be creative, only to find out that my motives were not the same as those of other stakeholders.

Maybe I'm eccentric, deranged, or simply difficult to get along with, but I like to think my intentions have always been pure.

Joining a band for me, was an opportunity to explore creative possibilities as a musician. It never occurred to me that many others saw playing music in public as one of several opportunities to play the mating game.

After working in such a team for a short while, I would notice the antics of my contemporaries and I would pull them up regarding attitudes that seemed inappropriate to me.

These differences of opinion almost always ended with me walking away from the team. Other interested parties looked on in horror, every time this happened.

A pillar of the record business was once asked if he had any advice for up-and-coming musicians. He summed up his thoughts in one word – *'Practise'*. If anyone asked me the same question, I would add two more words, which are *'And rehearse'*.

It might seem odd to any lay person, but I have met many people who describe themselves as musicians, who seem to loathe rehearsing.

In my humble opinion, practising and rehearsing are the two main forms of activity that any performing artist needs to be happy to live with. Facing audiences is the icing on the cake that has been baked, using those ingredients.

In with the new

I'm not a futurologist, but I've read the writings of someone who makes loads of money, advising big businesses about future trends.

I met someone else who described himself as such, many years ago in Lagos. He knew I was sceptical about his professed gift, so he had a word behind closed doors with the person who took me to see him, suggesting that I was malevolent and endowed with supernatural abilities. This was an accusation that wasn't to be taken lightly in a city that is a parallel universe at the best of times.

Psychic mediums have told me interesting things about my future, many of which have come to pass, further down the line, so I try to be careful in my thoughts about clairvoyants and their contemporaries.

You don't have to be clairaudient or anything like that to know that we are going through a moment of fundamental change right now, however.

Almost a hundred years ago, the motion pictures industry went through a massive change, from silent movies to the 'talkies', starting with Al Jolson in 'The Jazz Singer'.

Some silent movie performers were able to move into the 'talkies' era smoothly. In most cases, they were fortunate enough to have voices that were congruent with their faces. Many others fell by the wayside, mainly because they didn't sound right.

The Covid-19 disruption is turning the world upside down. Some folks want to clutch on the possibility that there will be an end to this saga, so we can all go back to doing things the same way as we did them before.

I'm looking in my imaginary crystal ball, and I can't see us going back to the old ways.

Hearing and adhering

In a conversation with a friend and her son (who was a child at the time), I was able to pass on a nugget of wisdom that someone had given me, years before.

The young person complained about having to spend time in a space with many grey-haired people of advanced ages.

I said to him *'You will be like them, one day'.* His mother immediately agreed with me. I sensed that the youngster heard my words but didn't understand what they meant.

When those words were uttered to me, I couldn't imagine what it would entail. Now that I'm getting closer to the actual experience, I think about my peers who will not know the feeling of being mature in years, in this lifetime.

I have many opportunities to reflect about choices and decisions made in my younger years. What would I have done differently? How can I apply the lessons I've learnt to new events as they arise?

Is it possible that folks of my generation were too docile and willing to accept the status quo as it was when we were young?

The Londoner in me remembers the inner-city riots of the early 1980s in England. Those who took part in the direct action in those days are now growing grey hairs if they are still around.

The Nigerian side of things was very different. In that context, the same generation had to live their young adult lives through harsh and repressive military suppression. This led to a brain drain mass migration to other countries which is directly affecting the governance and development of that nation at present.

Advancements in communications technology have enabled youngsters of today to pull together and take a stand, in ways that were unimaginable three decades ago.

Wisely, young Nigerian adults are seizing the moment to make their presence and feelings felt. When the dust settles, hopefully some of them will be interested enough in history, to find out and understand the reasons why their parents didn't do the same thing when they had that sort of energy.

A job becomes a chore.

I read an excerpt from the serialised memoirs of a key player in a British political scandal. There was a vignette therein featuring an encounter with an esteemed statesman.

The tale's narrator was of Russian extraction. He was introduced to the statesman, who was in a state of undress, waiting to receive some complementary therapy from the person they both knew.

After exchanging initial pleasantries, the statesman cut to the chase swiftly, in what he had to say.

Quoting him loosely, he said to the narrator. *'Leon Tolstoy was the greatest novelist of the 19th Century. Your people have great culture and traditions, but you allowed the Bolsheviks to destroy so many of them. In the end, you are Barbarians.'*

His words could be construed as harsh and impolite, and I'm sure the narrator found them offensive. He didn't have anything to say to the statesman in response, however. This is possibly because there was a grain of truth in the assertion.

A similar sequence of events to the one described by the statesman is currently playing itself out, closer to home.

Who will take responsibility for the collective nervous breakdown in Nigeria?

Tips about those quips

Recently, I listened to a public figure delivering a difficult message to a large audience. He was clearly uncomfortable. How was he going to appear to be accountable in a convincing manner?

With many years of experience in the public eye, this person also has the confidence of those who are well connected through access to an expensive education.

He relied on his loquacious nature to finesse his way through the situation, which was set up to seem like he was being held to account. In actual fact, questions were asked, and he answered them, but the questioners were not given airtime to follow up on his responses.

This encounter got me thinking about the way that so many people have been conditioned into conflating a plummy accent using a colourful vocabulary with wisdom, depth, and competence.

Many of us might be aware of class systems and their influence on our lives, but we don't know how to snap out of behavioural patterns that keep them in place

Home grown grass.

Back in the day, before the record business came up with a genre called 'World Music', which was used to describe any music that wasn't inspired by Anglo or Afro-American traditions, the industry's media used to call any music created by UK based artistes with an African sensibility, Home Grown.

An older musician was outspoken in his rejection of the term, mainly because he was aware of the way the term was used to describe a stimulant in the same circles. 'Home grown' products were regarded as inferior in quality when compared to the 'authentic' stuff, grown in other locations.

Several decades later, no one refers to home grown musicians or bands. In some cases, artists who were born and bred in London have relocated to various parts of the world, possibly aiming to gain credibility and badges of authenticity in the marketplace.

If an artist creates honest art, then surely it should be authentic, regardless of where he or she lives, not so?

Juwon's Bandcamp page goes live!

Occasionally, I'll let you know about new developments with my music. I have a homepage on Bandcamp.com for those of you who would like to buy my recordings. Bandcamp is a publishing platform for musicians.

The first lockdown phase gave me an opportunity to launch into a diverse range of activities, including this podcast series. I also present weekly vlog updates on Instagram, Facebook Live and Tik Tok. I was encouraged by a friend and colleague to create short songs to be performed in each podcast and vlog. There are quite a few new songs now.

Someone else suggested that I should perform a concert featuring these songs. I'm not ruling out the possibility that this will happen, but I was pleasantly surprised when I listened to some of the recordings. There is range and a variety of moods and feelings in the output.

Meanwhile, I knew I wanted to launch a Bandcamp page. Which recordings was I going to launch the page with? I thought of the song I contributed to Pitika Ntuli's online exhibition for the Melrose Gallery in South Africa as one option.

Debbie Golt of Resonance FM made two programmes about the exhibition, and I sent her two short song recordings from this series. Hearing the songs on the radio got me thinking about sharing them widely.

So here I am, letting you know about my Bandcamp homepage.

Please visit www.juwonogungbe.bandcamp.com/music to find out more.

Angles of a narrative

Years ago in Nigeria, I often noticed a quaint turn of phrase used as an abusive epithet by one person who was angry with someone else. 'You beast of no nation!', he or she would say.

One artist must have spent a considerable amount of time mulling over this jibe. It inspired him to write a song based on the premise that most politicians and ruling elites were not human. In his hypothesis, they were beasts from the spirit plane who assumed the physical attributes of people, on the earth plane. This was the reason why they were incapable of doing the right thing in their roles as leaders of nations.

The jury is still out, regarding the veracity of this notion. There are moments when political leaders appear to be so intoxicated by power however, that one starts wondering about it.

Is it possible that the political elite of the world's global north could be wolves, for example? Some of the shenanigans of the last few years are strong enough to summon up the imagery of the sort of savagery that one could associate with those creatures.

And what would be the equivalent in the global south? Could they be snakes?

Candlelight

I find wellness and well-being very interesting. Sometimes I read about a relatively obscure approach to the maintenance of good health, and I'm intrigued enough to want to find out more.

This was the way I came across the Metamorphic Technique. I found a broadsheet article interesting enough to want to make enquiries. I ended up having regular treatments for over ten years.

In the practice of the Metamorphic Technique, the practitioner uses a light, non-invasive touch on specific areas of the feet, hands and head while at the same time providing a space free from direction towards a particular outcome. An environment may then emerge in which it is acknowledged that the power and intelligence already inherent in the person is the best guiding factor for the unique life of the person.

The technique is related to Reflexology, but apparently simpler in practice. Why did I find it so attractive? I believe the sessions gave me time and space to focus on tuning into my essence. I was lucky to meet a practitioner who was well suited to dealing with my needs at that point in my life. The sessions came to an end when I went to work in the USA for protracted period. I felt the urge to turn a new leaf when I returned to London.

The practitioner and I were still in contact for a long while, but I never saw her in person again. Eventually, I learnt that she passed away, due to Covid-19. So, I want to thank her and pay tribute to her spirit.

I ain't playing

"The definition of insanity is doing the same thing over and over again and expecting different results", or so the saying goes...
I've tried various approaches in my creative practice through the years. After doing what I do for so long, I think I have a good idea about things that don't work for me.

I still have some energy and I'm compos mentis. It's time to do things differently.

To do so, I'm aligning myself with different sounds, shapes, ideas, and associates. Maybe I'm less approachable than before. Does this make me guilty of ghosting?

In changing my terms of reference, so much that used to matter to me is no longer relevant.

Someone sent me a link to a video clip of a solo piano recital. The pianist played several sonatas by Beethoven. I like some of this composer's output, but not everything.

Even though I was only vaguely interested in the pieces, the pianist kept my attention for over an hour. His technique was excellent, and he was emotionally committed to the music.

After a while, I found myself thinking about some of the creative choices made by the composer. None of the pieces was as striking or memorable as the *Moonlight Sonata*, but I realised that this was not important.

Artists are often expected to aim for hits. There is nothing wrong with hitting the jackpot.

An artistic product that isn't acknowledged as a blockbuster is just as valid as anything else. The composer had something to express, the performer found something to identify with and the resulting performance was engaging.

I would like to keep the noise out of my head that persuades me to want to "hit the spot".

Festive Event

At this time of the year, I am usually involved in organising, rehearsing, and performing events that feature lots of Christmas Carol singing, but 2020 is different, due to the disruptive influence of COVID 19.

It is fair to say that I miss the nativity plays, visits to care homes, singing at local authority events to switch on Christmas lights, Carols by Candlelight and Carol services. I do have a couple of online events this week, however.

Both events are somehow linked to the London borough of Ealing. The first one is a performance by Lyrical Voices – the Ealing Libraries Choir.

Singing in a group on Zoom is tricky, since there are issues with delay and latency. Lyrical Voices has soldiered on through the lockdowns and now we are used to hearing ourselves in a different way.

The second event is a workshop I'll be leading for Ealing Adult Learning. It's called *'Festive Singing for good cheer'* and it will focus on solo singing.

Time to reflect.

I get messages from peers and contemporaries, aiming to draw my attention to current affairs and cultural ideas. Most of the data is old news to me, possibly because I've always maintained an active interest in topical issues.

In several cases, these folks come across as deflated when they realise, they're telling me nothing new. When I explain about the terms of reference, I use for keeping tabs on things, they say I shouldn't expect them to have access to the same information, since their career paths are different to mine.

For a long time, I took pride in being tuned into the zeitgeist. The lockdown phases of 2020 have given me a new perspective, however.

Why have I invested so much time and energy in being aware of the outside world? What choices would I have made if I had focused more on my inner life?

I'm glad that I can make sense of life events because of observing others. Maybe there's a point one can reach where this becomes distractive.

I don't believe Christmas has been cancelled, even though I live in London, which is currently classified within Tier 4 of the efforts to curb the spread of the pandemic in England.

Yuletide, Winter solstice, Christmas, call it what you will, is a great time for looking within.

The best possible taste

The classical arts are usually associated with high minded ideals, such as refinement of style, class, and manners. Association with the music of courts and temples could be described as elitist, but it doesn't follow that folks who do so are more sophisticated or classy than others.

Many years ago, I went to party that was held on a boat on the Thames. It was probably hosted by an Arts funding organisation, or possibly an arts festival.

One of the guests was a well-known theatre director who shall remain nameless. I am an admirer of some of his work, so I took the opportunity say hello.

He was approachable and willing to have a chat, so I spoke to him about some of his productions that I had seen. One of these was of an opera and it was staged under the auspices of a leading opera company.

Eyebrows were raised when this project was mentioned. The director called a colleague hovering nearby to join in the conversation. He described his experience of working with the opera company as 'harrowing'.

The members of the company's orchestra were given particularly short shrift. To quote the director 'You could throw a live cow into the Orchestral pit, and it would be sent back to you as a carcass!'

I have heard tales from fellow artists about the director

himself being rather high maintenance to deal with, but I was gobsmacked by his story.

Updating customs

It was more than thirty years ago that Italy hosted the World Cup. The theme song recording for the event was Pavarotti's rendition of 'Nessun Dorma', from Puccini's last opera – 'Turandot'.

Pavarotti was already well known internationally, but the recording became an unusual chart hit. It was a neat and pure performance of an operatic aria that made no concessions to the sounds or trends of the time.

Nowadays, 'Nessun Dorma' is probably regarded as a pop song. A vast number of singers have trotted it out in performances in various settings. In 1990, it was thrilling to hear it on the radio, in all its grandeur. If Puccini had been on the Earth Plane, it's likely that he would have been proud of the moment.

Last night, I woke up and heard that recording echoing in my head. It made me think about stories and the way they are told.

Akin Euba, the composer and musicologist who passed away a few years ago, wrote about Yoruba Folk Opera, based on some of his research. My mother told me about performances of shows she remembered from her childhood. She sang some of the songs, but never told me whether she was involved in any productions in her community.

I'm not an aficionado of Yoruba folk opera, but I am aware of the building blocks or performative elements used to mount productions of such shows.

Now I'm wondering what would happen if the worlds of 'Nessun Dorma' and Yoruba folk opera were spliced together, to create a new updated genre.

I have a feeling there are still many untested choices to be made, with the potential to tug at collective heart strings.

Choices and impact

One night, several decades ago, I was on my way to a get together, round the corner from where I live. On the high street, I met a colleague who asked me where I was going. I told him I was going to a party. He asked if he could tag along. Since I knew he was familiar with some of the folks in the house where the party was happening, I said he could.

When we reached our destination, he met a young woman who lived in the house. By the end of the evening, it was clear that they were going to have a fling, at the very least.

In no time at all, I was attending birthday parties of someone who was born because of that encounter. The two parents were not an item for very long, but now their lives are linked forever, due to the conception and birth of their offspring.

What would have happened if I had said 'no' to my colleague that evening? It is possible that the parents could have met under other circumstances.

Sometimes, seemingly random events produce situations that couldn't have been planned for. People get diverted or distracted and end up having to go with the flow.

Being romantic about aesthetics

I might be veering close to telling the same stories repeatedly, but sometimes, a narrative sequence of events can be relevant to several situations.

Some years ago, I was a guest of an artist friend who lives in Bulawayo, Zimbabwe. I love Zimbabwe, but I find Bulawayo's atmosphere rather odd.

Because it was the homestead of Cecil Rhodes – the imperialist, Bulawayo has a unique layout as a city.

Rhodes was inspired by the grid like town planning of roads in many American cities, so Bulawayo's streets have that sort of structure.

My friend had a studio space within the city's main art gallery. I was lucky enough to be shown a lot of work in several rooms in the institution.

Most of the local artists had painted pictures that reminded me of the work of Edward Hopper and similar American visual artists. Yes, it is true that Bulawayo looks similar to American cities on a superficial level, but the people on the streets have very different ways of life to Americans.

Meanwhile, a British born artist of African heritage went to Bulawayo, possibly looking for inspiration. He came away with a striking visual vocabulary that captivated international audiences.

What role does mindset or perspective play in the effectiveness of communication?

Needs and acceptance

Once upon a time, I was a muse for a clothes designer. I know it's hard to imagine what it was like if you weren't around in those days, but I'm telling the truth.

The designer made African clothes. I would buy fabrics from various sources, take them to his atelier and he would come up with new ideas, inspired by my choices.

The arrangement we had was mutually beneficial. People in my line of work ordered outfits from the designer, and I had a striking image that worked in my favour, most of the time.

I had a few unpleasant experiences because of my look, however. One of these was in a most unusual setting.

I live in a part of North London that has a notable Turkish community. At the bottom of the high street, there used to be a Turkish restaurant that was renowned all over England for its interior design and cuisine.

On one occasion I went there for a takeaway meal. As I waited to collect my order, a man fixed a glare on me. He started a running commentary about the clothes I was wearing, like a mocking version of a fashion reporter in a television newsreel from the 1950s.

'Over coat with no lapels. Baggy trousers dragged in by the cat...' etc

His remarks became increasingly obnoxious and after a while, I had to ask him if he had a problem. We were both inside an exotic

Turkish restaurant, after all…

'*No*' He said. '*But you're dressed up all foreign*'.

'*So, what's the problem with that?*' I asked?

'*We're in England*' he said. At this point, my order had arrived, and he seemed like a thug who was looking for a punch up, so I took my meal and promptly left the restaurant.

There was a lot to unpick in the situation. The man spoke with a working-class North London accent, but his ethnicity was not English. I still don't know what to make of the experience.

Seeking approval.

In 2020, I released a single and an EP. The EP is called 'Glisten and Burn'.

Staying true to my calling as a singing theatre artist, the whole project tells a story that focuses primarily on Baron Samedi, one of the loas of the Voodoo faith.

In my sequence of events, Baron Samedi is busy dealing with requests for support and help from people on the Earth plane who are struggling to cope with the demands of the COVID-19 disruption. Obviously, the folks in need are seeking the Baron's approval.

Samedi is Saturday is a song that introduces the Baron to those who do not know him. This song was released as a single.

Interludes 1 & 2 are moments for the Baron's assistants to explain matters related to etiquette when he is being dealt with.

In the Family features a family calling on the Baron to save their patriarch, who is suffering in the throes of COVID 19, in an ICU unit.

G-nash, g-nash, g-nash tells a story of a cuckolded husband who used a charm on his wife that is called *Magun* by the Yorubas. The wife finds herself in a compromised situation and the husband is calling on the Baron to find a solution to their marital problem.

The Baron doesn't approve of too many things, so the problem scenarios are rather convoluted to sort out.

Visit my Bandcamp page for more information about the *'Glisten and Burn'* EP.

Are minds changing?

I'm enough of a realist to accept when a horse has bolted out of a stable, so to speak. This doesn't mean I won't sometimes reflect with fondness about times when the horse was still secure in its allocated space.

There was a time when folks mainly met each other face to face, in watering holes and eateries. In those days, we all developed and maintained social skills to an appreciable level. Yes, there were times when people spoke out of turn, or stepped out of line. There were bars where guys hurled stools at each other when it was closing time, but usually, a cadre of elders would intervene to make individuals understand where they went wrong when this happened.

In the age of social media interaction, people discovered they could treat others with disrespect, because they could hide behind their devices and say or do anything they liked.

Events of recent years in the politics of the USA took this sort of engagement into spaces that no one would have thought possible before.

We can't turn back the clock. Social skills are different to what they used to be. What can we do bring back civility and manners in the way we engage with each other, especially in public spaces?

Rapt attention

Today, I want to remember a dear friend. He was a talented actor who left the Earth plane at a very young age. I feel as if his spirit creeps up on me now and again. In those moments, I find myself reflecting about our years of early adulthood. Have I made the best use of the time since then?

One evening several decades ago, he and I went out on a pub crawl. We ended up in a well-known theatre pub, not far from where I live. Maybe we were drawn in by the live music we heard inside.

Onstage, in a central part of the main saloon, a singer sang for her supper. She sang jazz standards to an enthusiastic following. My friend and I were the only Black people in the pub at the time.

The audience cheered and clapped at the end of a number. I remember feeling neutral about the performance. I wasn't in the pub to hear a show, but at the same time, I was respectful enough of the performer's need to be listened to.

She started talking and mentioned that she had seen *Stormy Weather* – a film that featured Lena Horne and Bill 'Bojangles' Robinson. It was a film with an all-black cast. 'Isn't that wonderful?', the singer asked.

Suddenly, we felt like the whole room was staring at us. We didn't know where to look. The singer started singing another song.

I sensed that the singer was aiming to be generous and inclusive, but I felt uncomfortable, and I think my friend had similar feelings.

I guess terms of reference for being 'woke' have moved on quite a bit since those days.

Favours and the long game

An infamous provocateur once remarked that great surges in musical expression tend to happen in cultures that have been somehow traumatised. Music is supposed to function as an outlet for venting feelings about unfairness and calls for direct action.

I believe this person was correct, but I also think that folks in such situations sometimes become narcissistic about the potency of their musical gifts.

The Blues can be described as the original outlet that cousins across the pond had for expressing feelings of sorrow, depression, anger, etc. Coming from the voices of singers such as Ma Rainey, Bessie Smith, Robert Johnson, Muddy Waters, Nina Simone and from the instruments of Miles Davis, BB King and others, the output produces a similar sort of catharsis to that evoked by Greek tragic drama.

Nowadays, many would suggest that Hip hop does something similar. Maybe it does, but the work of the current crop of leading artists in that genre doesn't seem to pack the same sort of emotional punch. What happened along the way?

There is no doubt that there are still many issues to be resolved regarding race in the USA. Black Lives Matter wouldn't exist otherwise.

The pain and trauma experienced by Black folks shouldn't be measured for comparison. Each person processes trauma in his or her own way. Slavery and sharecropping are not prevalent in the USA at present as far as I know. I believe there is a direct link between those demoralising experiences and the Blues that we know and love.

Now that lives are more affluent and flexible, the music evokes different moods and atmospheres.

Samedi is Saturday

Just after the first wave of the pandemic, I released a single. It's called Samedi is Saturday and it's the opening track on my EP – 'Glisten and Burn'.

The Samedi referred to in the single's title is Baron Samedi – a spirit of the Voodoo faith. It is believed by followers of the faith that the Baron is at his most powerful on Saturdays, which happens to be the day in between the crucifixion of Christ – on Good Friday, and the Resurrection on Easter Sunday.

I was inspired to create a character study of the Baron partially because of the sound of my voice. I also wanted to draw attention to a mythical figure from an African derived belief system, albeit from a Diaspora perspective.

In my singing studies, I came across a song cycle by Ravel called *Don Quichotte a Dulcinea,* which was inspired by the well-known character from the literary output of Cervantes – one of the leading Spanish authors.

After learning the songs, to perform them in a concert, my singing teacher suggested that I should do some research into the character, who is associated with the word 'quixotic' in the English language.

Baron Samedi is nothing like Don Quixote, but he is colourful and expressive. He is also linked with matters pertaining to life and death, so I thought he would be interesting to spend some time with.

Farewell, addiction.

Like many others, I've been paying attention to the public discourse about a high-profile television interview that was broadcast in the USA and the UK.

As a UK citizen, I am conscious of attitudes around issues of class and race in this country. Most of the time, I choose to ignore the impact made on my own life by these notions, but the issue of that moment jogged my memory about an experience I had in the not-too-distant past.

An acquaintance of mine was in the frame for a job in the household of one of the top houses. He asked me to act as a referee for his application. I was to receive a phone call from someone and to answer some questions about his character and how long I had known him. I agreed to do so.

It might be worth mentioning that the job applicant was a black man.

At the appointed hour, the phone rang, and I had a conversation that seemed to be reasonable and cordial. The person at the other end asked about the job applicant and I did my utmost to present him in as favourable a light as possible.

A couple of days later, I heard from the applicant. He was told that his application was unsuccessful. The reason given to him by the person employed by the top house was that I had said he was unsuitable for the job!

There was nothing I could say to convince the applicant that he had been told a lie. Our friendship hasn't recovered from this event.

In my opinion, it is easy for such organisations to claim they have exemplary diversity policies, but if they are so quick to tell lies about people they haven't even met face to face, why should they be trusted in what they have to say about a black or mixed race person who marries into the family of their employer?

What does the image say to you?

A psychic medium was asked about the prospects in office for the current president of the USA. She closed her eyes and after a while, said she could see the vision of a beautifully ornate grandfather clock. Considering the age range of the person in question, this made sense.

In her interpretation, the medium expressed concern about the fact that the clock wasn't keeping time. In other words, the hands for telling time were still.

She wondered aloud whether this feature in the image was linked to the statesman's health. The absence of ticking sounds made her mention his heart.

I was inspired to think about what the image meant to me. There is no doubt in my mind that a grandfather clock represents history, tradition and antiquity. The statesman is an old hand at dealing with global politics.

The lack of ticking and stillness of the hands or arrows speaks to me of timelessness. This does not mean the person in question will be stopped short. It could mean he isn't futuristic in his thinking, however.

Reserving the right to morph

In the early days of my career, I did a lot of learning on the job in performances. Then I reached a point where I wanted to extend my expressive and creative range, so I attended a conservatoire.

Adapting to the institution's ethos was demanding, and this was in an era when diversity issues were not high on the priority lists of such establishments.

I invited friends, relatives, and associates to attend end of term concerts and the first one was particularly tricky.

Some of my folks were triggered emotionally when they saw and heard me performing contemporary art music, surrounded by musicians of other backgrounds.

Nothing untoward happened during the concert, but afterwards I had to accept some browbeating from some of my invitees.

Other musicians present who happened to be black and studying in the institution were waylaid and harangued for the choices they had made.

Years later, some of those who reacted adversely had the grace to admit that they had overstepped the mark.

Nowadays, it's not unusual to see young people of African descent, carrying orchestral instruments, or indeed playing them in concert halls.

Who would have known we would live to see these developments?

Authenticity from Africa

Thumbing through pages of an old diary as you do, I came across a name and number that got me excited.

I had a phone number for Ambrose Campbell. Vague memories came to mind of the day when I met him, in the lobby of a rehearsal room studio. We must have had a good rapport, because he gave me his phone number, but at that point in time, I didn't know who he was, so I didn't try to stay in touch.

By the time I realised the error of my ways, I was much more aware of Mr Campbell and his talent. He remains one of the best examples of an African musician based in a Diaspora community who had a direct influence on the contemporary music in the land of his forebears.

Mr Campbell made a recording of a reggae song that used the chord progression of *'Hey Jude'* by The Beatles. He sang the song in Yoruba.

A much-loved purveyor of Juju music was moved to lift Ambrose Campbell's idea wholesale, recording the same song without the reggae rhythm section. If you hear both recordings, you will know that Campbell came up with the idea.

Ambrose Campbell was based in London when he made his recording. If I had been aware of who I was talking to, all those years ago in the rehearsal studio lobby, I would have been able to find out his opinion about being imitated so closely.

I have also met the Juju music legend in my travels, and he is a genuinely nice man.

Narratives have been peddled by record businesspeople about how inauthentic music made by London based Africans is, when it is compared to music made in Africa.

What does the Ambrose Campbell story have to teach us?

Discoveries about Destiny

I want to remember someone who had dreams that were not meant to materialise. Not on this plane, anyway.

Many years ago, I was aware of Winnie Mandela as a leading activist against apartheid in South Africa before I heard of her husband.

I'm not ashamed to say that I first heard of her ex-husband through the pop song recorded by The Special AKA – *'Free Nelson Mandela'*.

The singer who sang on the recording didn't stay in the group for long. After he left, there were several high-profile stadium concerts where the song was sung by other singers, including someone who I got to know quite well, who happened to be a Black South African.

He was a music student in a leading University of London College, and he got the opportunity to sing the protest song to thousands of listeners.

Shortly after that experience, we toured together in Sardinia with a men's choral group. We shared a lot of knowledge as we travelled to shows in remote villages in a minibus.

I still remember a song in Zulu that he taught us on the way, even though it was several decades ago.

The roads leading to our destinations were very narrow and in many cases on the edges of hills and mountains. There were times when I felt unsafe as we made our way back and forth.

On one occasion, we saw the outcome of a ghastly accident that happened on one of those narrow roads. It was upsetting, to say the least.

Nevertheless, we all survived the dangers of the narrow mountain roads and returned home to London. Sadly, that was the last time I saw the fellow I'm thinking of.

Not too long after that time, I heard he was a casualty in a road accident in South Africa. His life's work was already completed. I'm grateful for the memories.

Hearing Voices

Many years ago, I sang the title role in Verdi's opera based on 'the Scottish play' by Shakespeare, for a small training company. The production was in the original language – Italian, and it was double cast. The other person singing my role was a retired Italian banker who had started out as a professional singer in his youth.

The process felt daunting in the beginning. Each time we sang through a scene, I felt I was going to be compared unfavourably with a native Italian speaker, who was also much more aware of the singing tradition.

Verdi's music was great fun to get immersed in, so practising didn't feel like a chore. Going through the role with my teacher, after a while she noticed that I had unconsciously picked up stylistic features from listening to my colleague from the opposite cast.

I came from behind in that process to deliver a portrayal of the character that seemed to hit the spot at that stage in my development as a singing theatre artist.

It was one of several occasions where I was able to prove to myself that I was capable of functioning well, outside of my comfort zone.

In retrospect, I can also see that it was my ego that I was struggling with, in the beginning, but it was also my ego that fuelled me with the determination to deal well with the challenge.

Light and the downside

Like a snow globe, our lives have been given a good old shake, over the last year (2020). Now it's time to watch the snowflakes settling. One can only hope the outcome is a pretty picture.

Even if the picture ends up being beautiful, there are details to be considered.

Are there elements of the way life used to be, that need to be reactivated? And what of the things that ought to be discarded?

I'm reminded of a visit to the aquarium in Sydney, Australia, where there was a section featuring stingrays and man rays. The tanks were massive – larger than many rooms and there was a corridor one could walk through that was transparent, with these huge tanks on either side. It was amazing to see such big sea creatures at close quarters.

The present moment gives me a similar feeling to the one I got after walking through a corridor of that sort. I feel like a speck in the eyes of nature. But one must move forward with integrity.

Integrity is personal, meaning different things to different people. An inventory of values could be useful, as one emerges from the stillness.

Gliding with Swans

I love Motown music as much as the next person. There will always be a space in my heart for the folks who created those sounds and so many indelible memories.

But I hear many different languages and dialects within music. My tastes are eclectic.

For a long time, I got a special kick out of hearing the songs of Kurt Weill, performed by singers who know more about the world of his imagination than I do.

Back in the day, I wasn't supposed to mention this in polite society. It was seen to be too far removed from the subculture I associated with.

Then I discovered Milva - an Italian singer with tremendous expressive range, which she used to astounding effect in performing songs by Astor Piazzolla – the Argentine composer.

Milva and Pizzolla inspired me to dare to be different. They sowed seeds of adventure in my heart.

Today, I heard that Milva has passed away, aged 81. I can hear her voice ringing as I write these words.

I recommend the live album she recorded with Piazzolla - *'Live at the Bouffes Nord'* , as essential listening. It might not be your cup of tea, but it is certainly mine.

As her soul glides away, I want to say 'thank you' to Milva, for the music and the inspiration.

Perception and Baggage

In my artistic journey, I have maintained a social network of creative associates who work in a wide range of art forms. Naturally, many of them are of African or Caribbean descent. We kept an eye out for each other, celebrating successes and providing support in hours of need. Film launches, show openings, exhibition private viewings were part of our regular social whirl.

When things started picking up for me, some of my fellow artists from disciplines other than my own would sometimes attend my concerts, to find out what I was up to. We were all young things, with bright hopes.

I remember one occasion when such a person came to a show of mine. After the show he said to me 'Juwon, you'll need to change your name'.

I found this statement puzzling, just the same as when someone I was seeing said, I shouldn't expect to go too far with my creative practice, because of the darkness of my skin, compared to the lightness of those black people who occupied the spotlight in those days.

Here we are, several decades later and dark-skinned folks with unmistakeably African names are gaining access to all sorts of spaces that were seemingly out of bounds in those days.

I wonder how I would have felt if I had changed my name, or tried to lighten my skin tone to receive acceptance or validation from others?

Experience and Process

Sometimes, a person finds his or her way into securing a monopoly in a situation. When this happens, he or she can choose to handle responsibility with tact, fairness, and good grace, or to go for other options.

It has been said on many occasions that *'no condition is permanent'*. This statement could be debatable, but often, it turns out to be true.

Feathering the nest for the benefit of cronies and oneself is gratifying in the short term. Anyone who lives long enough will know the feeling of looking back wistfully at moments in time when opportunities and access were more readily available.

Sleaze and corruption in political circles are often taken for granted, but there are others who set up organisations and structures that do similar things with taxpayers' money and not much is said about them.

In the fullness of time however, the moment comes when positions have to be given up and the reins of influence and in many cases, affluence are relinquished.

This side of human behaviour can be found across cultures, creeds, ages, genders, and similar other categories. We are all works in progress.

Ode to an enduring friendship

This friend of mine was amply proportioned and liked his food. On one occasion he told me about a caregiver who frequently fed him with highly calorific food in his childhood. The habit remained with him throughout his life.

In New York, we met in a Cuban Chinese restaurant. My friend ordered a platter of broccoli that looked like a full standard sized tray. This was accompanied by a huge bowl of rice, on which he sprinkled almonds. The meat dish was still to arrive. It was an enlightening spectacle, observing him eat every single morsel of the food he ordered.

Then there was the time in London when he asked me to take him to a Nigerian restaurant. In those days, there was a reputable one close to Oval Cricket Ground. On arrival, my friend wanted me to tell him in detail about all the items on the menu. As the host in this situation, I was expected to foot the bill.

He looked at the starters and asked me about pepper soup. I advised him against ordering it, because he was of Afro-American heritage and I'm not aware of exceptionally piquant dishes in the cuisine of the American South. My friend accused me of being a cheapskate and not wanting to pay a large bill. I relented and let him have the pepper soup. He took one spoonful and looked me in the eye, saying *'I know you brought me here to make me suffer'.*

Then we argued over the main courses. He said, *'I want some Amala with beans.'* I objected, explaining that these dishes are not eaten together. It was a memorable evening, and we had a lot of fun.

Of my parents' generation, but from a different part of the African Diaspora, he wore baggy clothes that looked African. There were several occasions when folks we met asked if he was my father.

But now all the japes and fun are over as I found out this week that he passed away. My friend offered me a lot of mentoring through the years. I want to thank his larger-than-life spirit, wherever he might be, for the guidance he gave me.

About The Author

Juwon Ogungbe

Out of isolation comes connection, creativity and growth'.

A London based composer and singer, Juwon Ogungbe started making episodes of Multiverse – his podcast series, during the pandemic lockdowns. All Roads Lead to Peace is a collection of Multiverse episodic scripts.

Several years before the COVID pandemic, Juwon found himself in a similar situation in the USA, working in a university and living in isolation. Attending a psychic fayre, a medium told him 'You could write a cool book about your experiences', thereby giving him the inspiration for the book's title.

Using his skills as an erstwhile newspaper columnist, blogger, opera librettist and song lyricist, Juwon has now written, recorded, and presented almost 200 episodes of Multiverse. Creating the series has become a weekly ritual in his life, lasting for four years. Visit https://juwonogungbe.com and follow Juwon Ogungbe on Spotify to hear more podcast episodes, recordings, and playlists.

Printed in Poland
by Amazon Fulfillment
Poland Sp. z o.o., Wrocław